Warm summers and mild wi
Mediterranean Sea give this
of originality and raw beauty
music, cuisine and performa
people with a passion for foo
part of life, and small shops, k
bring constant new ideas to
flavour of Barcelona, bring a s............., ...

CITIx60: Barcelona explores the Catalan capital and the second largest city of Spain in five aspects, covering architecture, art spaces, shops and markets, eating and entertainment. With expert advice from 60 stars of the city's creative scene, this book guides you to the real attractions of the city for an authentic taste of Barcelona life.

Contents

Before You Go

BASIC INFO

Currency
Euro (EUR/€)
Exchange rate: €1 : $1.2

Time zone
GMT +1
DST +2

DST begins at 0200 (local time) on the last Sunday of March and ends at 0300 (local time) on the last Sunday of October.

Dialling
International calling: +34
Citywide: 93

Weather (avg. temperature range)
Spring (Mar–May): 10–19°C / 50–66°F
Summer (Jun–Sep): 20–28°C / 68–82°F
Autumn (Oct–Nov): 12–20°C / 54–68°F
Winter (Dec–Feb): 5–14°C / 41–57°F

USEFUL WEBSITES

Citywide public transport advisor
www.tmb.cat/en

Pocket Wifi
www.wifivox.com

EMERGENCY CALLS

Ambulance / Fire
061 / 080

Police
092

Embassies / consulates
China   +34 93 25 47 070
Japan   +34 93 28 03 433
France   +34 93 27 03 000
Germany   +34 93 29 21 000
UK   +34 93 36 66 200
US   +34 93 28 02 227

AIRPORT EXPRESS TRANSFERS

El Prat (T1) <–> pl. Catalunya (Aerobús A1)
Bus / Journey: every 5–10 min / 35 min
From El Prat – 0535–0105
From Plaza Catalunya – 0500–0030
One-way: €5.90
www.aerobusbcn.com

El Prat (T2) <–> Passeig de Gràcia
Trains / Journey: every 30 min / 25 min
From Aeropuerto or Passeig de Gràcia Station – 0532–2338
One-way: €4.20 or €1.02 with T10 multi-trip ticket
www.renfe.com

PUBLIC TRANSPORT IN BARCELONA

Metro
Bus & NitBus
Train
Tram
Taxi
Funicular

Means of Payment
T10 travel card* (cost per card varies per zone)
Credit cards at Metro ticket vending machine
Cash

*Each trip includes three bus, metro, train or tramway transfers made within 75 min.

BANK HOLIDAYS

January	1 New Year's Day, 6 Epiphany
March/April	Good Friday, Easter Monday
May	1 Labour Day
May/June	Whit Monday
June	24 Sant Joan
August	15 Assumption Day
September	11 Diada
October	12 Columbus Day
November	1 All Saints' Day
December	8 Immaculate Conception, 25 Christmas Day

Cultural institutions and shops might be closed or have varied opening hours on public holidays.

FESTIVALS / EVENTS

January
080 Barcelona Fashion (also in June/July)
www.080barcelonafashion.cat

March
Mutek
www.mutek.org

May
LOOP Barcelona
www.loop-barcelona.com
OFFF Barcelona
www.offf.ws
Primavera Sound
www.primaverasound.es

June
Barcelona Design Week
www.barcelonadesignweek.com
Pride Barcelona
www.pridebarcelona.org
Sónar
www.sonar.es

August / September
Festa Major de Gràcia
www.festamajordegracia.cat
Festes de la Mercè
www.spanish-fiestas.com
Swab
swab.es

October / November
Barcelona Jazz festival
www.jazz.barcelona
L'Alternativa Film Festival
www.alternativa.cccb.org

December
Festivalet
www.festivalet.org

Event days vary by year. Please check for updates online.

UNUSUAL OUTINGS

Barcelona Architecture Walks
www.barcelonarchitecturewalks.com

Culinary Backstreets
www.culinarybackstreets.com

Hidden City Tours
hiddencitytours.com

My Favourite Things
www.myft.net

Rainbow Barcelona Tours
rainbowbarcelona.es

Ride or Die Bike Rental and Tours
www.rideordie.es

SMARTPHONE APPS

Hidden spots discovered
BCN Paisatge

Public transport in control
TMB

Bike routes, locator & available bikes/docks
Bicing

REGULAR EXPENSES

Single public transport ticket
€2.20 (Metro)

Domestic / International mail (standard postcards)
€0.42 / €0.90

Gratuities
Diners: optional 5% for waitstaff & round up to whole amount for bartenders
Hotels: €1@bag for the porter, €1 daily for cleaners
Licensed taxis: round up to whole amount

*Look out for pickpockets. They find targets in subways or come on bicycles.

Count to 10

What makes Barcelona so special?

Illustrations by Guillaume Kashima aka Funny Fun

Life in Barcelona is a rich tapestry of traditions and tastes brimming with creativity. Niche magazines, artisanal food and drink, modernist architecture and contemporary art thrives, making the trend-ready city a pleasure for the senses. Whether you are on a one-day stopover or a week-long stay, see what Barcelona creatives consider essential to see, taste, read and take home from your trip.

1

Architecture

Eixample (#3)
by Ildefons Cerdà

La Sagrada Familia (#9)
by Antoni Gaudí

Santa Maria del mar Church
by Berenguer de Montagut

Palau Baró de Quadras
by Josep Puig i Cadafalch

Palau de la Música Catalana
by Lluís Doménech i Montaner

Parc dels Auditoris
*by Foreign Office Architects
(Alejandro Zaera-Polo & Farshid Moussavi)*

Torre Diagonal Zero Zero
by EMBA

5

International Reads

La Central
www.lacentral.com

Loring Art
www.loring-art.com

Fatbottom (#32)
www.fatbottombooks.com

Liberia Gigamesh
www.gigamesh.com

Freaks Books
www.freaks-books.com

6

Contemporary Art & Crafts

CCCB (#21)
www.cccb.org

MACBA (#13)
www.macba.cat

Arts Santa Monica
artssantamonica.gencat.cat/en/

Hangar (#18)
hangar.org/en

Duduá
duduadudua.blogspot.com

Angels Barcelona
www.angelsbarcelona.com

Swab
swab.es

Museu de la Xocolata
www.museuxocolata.cat

7

Homegrown Magazines

apartamento
Everyday life interiors biannual
www.apartamentomagazine.com

THE PLANT
Greenery & art biannual
http://theplantmagazine.com

METAL
Fashion & arts biannual
revistametal.com

Openhouse
Creative lifestyle & travel biannual
quaderns.coac.net

Fucking Young!
Men's fashion biannual
fuckingyoung.es

8
Markets

Mercat del Ninot
Fresh produce & Jabugo ham
www.mercatdelninot.com

Lost & Found Market Barcelona
Secondhand market
lostfoundmarket.com

Mercat de Sant Antoni
Odds & ends
www.mercatdesantantoni.com

SusiSweetdress Market
Vintage dresses
www.susisweetdress.com

Mercat del Clot
Bizarre souvenirs
www.mercatdelclot.net

Els Encants Vells (#10)
www.encantsbcn.com

Mercat de la Boquería (#36)
www.boqueria.info

9
Mementos

Catalan designer clothes
by Antonio Miró or Sita Murt

Porró (wine pitcher)
Mercat de Sagrada Familia
www.mercatsagradafamilia.com

Traditional Catalan espadrilles
La Manual Alpargatera
lamanualalpargatera.es

A Cobi figure
El Coleccionista
c/Enric Granados 102, L'Eixample

Olive oil (Siurana origin)
Oro Líquido
www.oroliquido.es

10
Leisure

Beach Picnic
Nova Icaria / Bogatell

**Longboard skating
around the city**
Inercia Shop
www.inercia-shop.com

Explore the city
Bike along coastal line
from W Hotel to Parc del Fòrum

See the Castellers
pl. Sant Jaume, El Gòtic

Eat ice cream in summer
Gelateria Italiana
Pl. de la Revolució, Vila de Gràcia

A walk around Montjuïc
See Castell de Montjuïc, The
Olympic Ring, Botanical Gardens,
Cementiri de Montjuïc

Icon Index

 Opening hours   Admission

 Address   Facebook

 Contact   Website

 Remarks

 Scan QR codes to access Google Maps and discover the area around each destination. Internet connection required.

60x60

60 Local Creatives x 60 Hotspots

From vast cityscapes to the smallest snippets of conversation, there is much to inspire creative urges in Barcelona. 60x60 points you to 60 haunts where 60 arbiters of taste develop their nose for the good stuff.

Landmarks & Architecture

SPOTS · 01 – 12

Experience a charming blend of old with new. Start at Eixample to tour modernista architecture before taking a ramble to the labyrinth old town.

Cultural & Art Space

SPOTS · 13 – 24

Be inspired by the dynamic melting pot of artistic disciplines, from movement to sound arts. Creative spaces and art factories offer cultural programmes all day long.

Markets & Shops

SPOTS · 25 – 36

Let independent boutiques and century-old family businesses greet you with proud selections, then find Catalan wine and choice food at groceries and markets.

Restaurants & Cafés

SPOTS · 37 – 48

Start your day with a pre-lunch vermouth before hitting the famed tapas — rich cacophonies of tasty small dishes. Don't miss traditional Catalan stews and sauces.

Nightlife

SPOTS · 49 – 60

Bask in Barcelona's sunset on a high ground, then go bar-hopping or watch a play after dark. Pubs and bars offer roots, reggae, soul, techno, flamenco and Spanish Copla, among others.

Landmarks & Architecture

Catalan modernism, new architecture and Barcelona's skyline

Barcelona's distinctive architecture offers an ideal way to contemplate the city. Although new designs like Torre Agbar by Jean Nouvel and Els Encants Vells (#10) by local practice b720 are slowly transforming Barcelona's skyline, churches, mansions and factories from the 19th and 20th century remain a main attraction of this landscape. La Sagrada Familia (#9) by Antoni Gaudí, still an incomplete construction after 130 years, and Ildefons Cerdà's visionary Eixample grid street plan (#3) are icons and cannot be missed, but sniff out more hidden treasures, around the neighbouring districts, including el Gòtic, el Born, el Raval, Vila de Gràcia (#2) and Sant Antoni, and the earlier works of Gaudí at El Dipòsit de les Aigües (#1) and Parc de la Ciutadella (#5). If you have only one day, take the "Modernist Route (map D)" to track down the most iconic examples of Catalan Modernism, such as Casa Batlló and Casa Milà (also known as 'La Pedrera'), both Gaudí masterpieces, and other works by Josep Puig i Cadafalch and Lluís Doménech i Montaner.

Albert Ibanyez
Graphic designer

Born in Barcelona, currently working freelance on projects related to art, editorial, typography and web design with clients like Fundació Antoni Tàpies and ELISAVA.

Vila de Gràcia
015

CrousCalogero
Design agency

A Barcelona-based consultancy founded in 2009 by Francesc Crous and Alessandro Calogero who met at the Innovation Lab at Roca. We are also professors at EINA Barcelona.

Carles Enrich Giménez
Architect & interior designer

I combine research, teaching and practice in my own studio and develop alternative ways to unify houses with the city. I like to see architecture with a multidisciplinary look.

Dipòsit de les Aigües
014

Eixample
016

Enric Soldevila
Creative director, TBWA Amsterdam

I worked as a 3D artist, graphic designer, art director and teacher. I did an around-the-world trip with a stop in the Tokyo jail and love to ride my motorbike as fast as I can.

Parc de la Ciutadella
018

Karlota Laspalas
Fashion designer

Fashion designer born in Pamplona, 1981. My work is a constant observation and experimentation of human identity, exploring our fears, longings and hopes.

Isa Rodríguez
Founder, INDASTUDIO BCN

Interior designer and creative director of INDASTUDIO BCN. Graduated from Bau Design College and previously worked with Sandra Taruella and Isabel López.

Bunkers del Carmel
017

Disseny Hub Barcelona
019

Max-o-matic
Designer & illustrator

I'm Máximo Tuja, a collage artist and fanzine lover based in Barcelona since 2002. In my spare time I play with my son, run middle distances and make (horrible) music with friends.

Pavelló Mies van der Rohe
021

Isahac Oliver Ponce
Creative director, &Rosàs

I'm 35 years old, married and a brand new father. I have been working in advertising for 13 years and right now am the executive creative director of new advertising adventure, &Rosàs.

Frank Plant
Artist

I'm an American sculptor based in Barcelona for 14 years. I do drawings in steel plate and bar that observe objects and social dynamics.

Carretera de les Aigües
020

La Sagrada Familia
022

Borja Martínez
Founder, Lo Siento

My name is Borja Martínez, founder of Lo Siento studio in Barcelona. Our projects are mainly related to culture, music and food. We love to eat and take humour very seriously.

La Barceloneta
025

Atipus
Graphic design studio

We are a Barcelona-based studio founded in 1998, working across a variety of media and fields. We believe in conceptual, creative and simple design.

UnitedFakes
Multimedia design studio

We are a multidisciplinary team who likes to switch roles in every project. As much as we use computers daily, we still love to get our hands dirty.

Els Encants Vells
024

Parc Güell
028

① Dipòsit de les Aigües
Map F, P.108

Sitting discreetly inside Universitat Pompeu Fabra's Ciutadella's campus is "The Water Tank," the university's main library. Its name originates from the site's earlier incarnation as a reservoir for Parc de la Ciutadella's (#5) cascade and irrigation, a Joseph Fontserè project on which Antoni Gaudí (1852–1926) assisted as a student architect in 1876. Said to be a copy of Italy's Piscina Mirabilis but with pool built on the rooftop, the building is now a fortified hypostyle hall accommodating a rich book collection and study areas comprising 7,850sqm. Enter through the entrance at the adjacent Jaume I block, the library is open to all visitors.

🕐 0800–0130 (M–F), 1000–2100 (Sa–Su, & P.H.) 🏠 Ramon Trias Fargas, 25–27, Vila Olímpica, 08005 📞 +34 93 54 22 000 🔗 www.upf.edu/campus/en/ciutadella/aigues.html

"In the university's cafeteria there are sandwiches for €1 and coffee for 50 cents."
– Albert Ibanyez

2 Vila de Gràcia

Map C, P.103 / Map D, P.104

Vila de Gràcia is a hipster barrio buzzing with the yesteryear charm of an older independent municipality. In between the area's low-rise buildings, roughly bounded by avinguda Diagonal to its south, find character shops like Duduá and BOO. Hit bars and terraces along carrer de Verdi or visit Bodega Bonavista at carrer de Bonavista 10 for local artisanal beers and Catalan wines. If you come in late August, be sure to join "Festes Major," where decoration, live music, pyrotechnics and cultural entertainment fill the streets.

🖉 Duduá: http://duduadudua.
blogspot.com,
BOO: www.boobcn.com,
Festa Major de Gràcia: www.
festamajordegracia.cat

"Take a walk through the small squares in the dense 19th century urban structures across from plaça de la Vila, the Central Market or plaça de la Virreina."

– Carles Enrich Giménez

3 Tibidabo (Eixample)
Map J, P.111

If you're coming in by air, the most noticeable feature looking down is the city centre's extensive grid pattern, which urban planner Ildefons Cerdà (1815–76) drew up more than 150 years ago. Cerdà's gift for Barcelona's people were broad streets and square blocks with chamfered corners allowing considerable sunlight, high visibility and ventilation in the extended space – a blessing for townsfolk that had been packed into an overcrowded city experiencing rapid population growth. The area is known today as Eixample, which is Catalan for "extension."

URL Any Cerdà: www.anycerda.org
🔗 Tibidabo Amusement Park: www.tibidabo.cat

"Find the best view of Barcelona at the Tibidabo Park."
– CrousCalogero

4 Bunkers del Carmel
Map C, P.103

Once the core of Barcelona's defences against 1936–9 fascist aerial attacks, the Spanish Civil War bunker is now a hush-hush spot to savour the city. Enjoy a picnic, with music, friends or loved ones, or just soak up the sun from this lofty point in the hilly neighbourhood of Carmel. Moving up one of the steepest slopes in Barcelona, however, requires some strength. Take a 30-minute walk uphill from Guinardó Station (L4), or take bus 119 from El Coll Station (L5) uphill and find the little path that leads to the top.

🏠 c/Marià Lavernia, 08032
URL www.bunkers.cat/en/

"In the 1950s, many Spanish immigrants built their houses here which developed into barracas (favela). Now you can find the best views of the city here."

– Enric Soldevila, TBWA Amsterdam

⑤ Parc de la Ciutadella
Map F, P.108

Take a break from the city with a leisurely picnic on the parterre or row a boat among wild geese and ducks in the great lake. Beautifully landscaped in 1872 by Josep Fontseré (1829–97) for the bourgeoisie, Ciutadella Park distinguishes itself with numerous Catalan sculptures, the lake, fountains, rich vegetation and architecture. Central to the design is the Baroque Cascade, alongside the shade house, the Greenhouse and a turreted castle created for the Universal Exhibition in 1888. The park is also home to the Parliament of Catalonia and Barcelona Zoo, to its south.

 ⓒ *1000–2000 daily (mid-Mar to mid-Sep), –1800 daily (mid-Sep to mid-Mar)* 🏠 *pg. Picasso, 21, la Ribera, 08003* 🔗 *Boat hire: €2–10, Zoo: €19.90/11.95*

"Enjoy a pleasant walk admiring wonderful buildings, fountains and lakes designed by architects as important as Domenech i Montaner and Gaudí."

– Karlota Laspalas

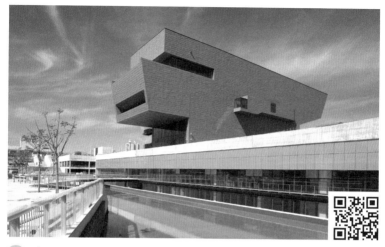

6 Disseny Hub Barcelona (DHUB)

Map B, P.102

The city's new design centre emphasises public space as much as an area to display design works. In contrast to the Jean Nouvel-designed Torre Agbar at Plaça de les Glòries, the zinc-clad angular edifice houses an auditorium and temporary exhibition halls over seven floors, and extends underground to host the main exhibition hall, a public library, restaurants and main offices, all lit by skylight. Disseny Hub Barcelona (DHUB) intends to exhibit far-reaching programmes across fashion, graphics, space and product design.

🕐 1600-2030 (M), 1000- (Tu-Su)
🏠 pl. de les Glòries Catalanes, 37-38, el Parc i la Llacuna del Poblenou, 08018 📞 +34 93 25 66 700
🔗 www.dissenyhubbarcelona.cat

"Stroll around the outside space with its lake and ground lighting effects, then visit the Agbar Tower and the new Encants Market (#10)."

– Isa Rodríguez, INDASTUDIO BCN

7 Carretera de les Aigües
Map J, P.111

Sitting in the hills of Collserola, Carretera de les Aigües is a wide, flat unpaved path, where water pipes used to run. With spectacular views of Barcelona and its coastline, the track is a natural hot spot for a morning jog or bike ride with fresh air and zero cars. Access the trail by taking FGC (S1/S2) to Peu del Funicular, then change to the Vallvidrera line and alight at Carretera de les Aigües station. If you are keen to walk, the meandering path will guide you to Tibidabo, though it gets much steeper near the hilltop. Those avoiding the climb should leave at pla dels Maduixers and return to the city through avinguda Tibidabo.

"If you have your running shoes with you, put them on and go there. You have about 20km to train for your next race or just to disconnect from everything."
– Máximo Tuja aka Max-o-matic

8 Pavelló Mies van der Rohe
Map G, P.109

Erected for the 1929 Barcelona International Exhibition, the German Pavilion by Ludwig Mies van der Rohe (1886-1969) portrayed the new Germany as a prospering democratic country, with an open plan, proportional interplay between interior and exterior space, reflection and actuality, the man-made and the natural. The infamous Barcelona Chair was also created as part of the design. The original pavilion, however, was removed in 1930 after the fair's closure, and was only rebuilt in 1986.

🕐 1000-2000 daily (Mar-Oct), -1800 (Nov-Feb) 💲 €5/2.60/Free for 16- 🏠 av. Francesc Ferrer i Guàrdia, 7, La Font de la Guatlla, Montjuïc, 08038 📞 +34 93 21 51 011 URL www.miesbcn.com 🔗 Cash only

"Near Montjuïc you can admire this 20th century landmark, a result of the painstaking reconstruction carried out in the 1980s."

– Isahac Oliver Ponce, &Rosàs

9 La Sagrada Família
Map D, P.105

Since 1883, the church of La Sagrada Família has been a grand work in progress. Architect Antoni Gaudí (1852–1926), a religious man with a love for nature, had envisaged the design a catechistic explanation of the teachings of the Gospels and the Church. Complex structures loaded with symbolic details were planned, including many parts that the architect knew he would not live to see built. In fact, only the first bell tower of the Nativity façade, dedicated to Barnabas the Apostle, was completed within Gaudí's lifetime. To skip the queue, buy advance tickets online.

🕐 0900–1800 daily (Nov-Feb), –1900 (Mar), –2000 (Apr-Sep), –1400 (Dec 25&26, Jan 1&6)
💲 €15/Free for 10- 🏠 c/Mallorca, 401, Dreta de l'Eixample, 08013 URL www.sagradafamilia.org
🔗 Guided tour (incl. entry): €29/24/22

"The height of Gaudi's creativity and genius are captured in this monumental masterpiece."

– Frank Plant

10 Els Encants Vells
Map B, P.102

In keeping with the traditions of this long-es-
tablished flea market – Barcelona's biggest –
local design firm b720 adhered to the concept
of a meandering open space. Rag-lovers can
poke around Moroccan and gypsy stalls, which
sell everything from flooring to coffin keys,
venturing from pitch to pitch via a swirling
walkway that connects the space. A giant canopy suspended by metal casings protects from
glaring midday sun but not from pickpockets
– pay close attention to your belongings during
a visit.

🕐 0900–2000 (M, W, F–Sa)
🏠 B/w c/Castillejos, 158 & av. Meridiana, 08013
📞 +34 93 24 52 299
URL www.encantsbcn.com

*"Els Encants Vells is one of the three important
new architectural features in Glòríes."*

– Borja Martínez, Lo Siento

11 La Barceloneta

Map H, P.110

Narrow streets, eclectic bodegas and the smell of sea salt in the air – the seaside enclave next to Barceloneta beach has retained its charm as an old fishermen's village. Sample seafood from the local auction sale prepared fresh each day, along with which authentic tapas are famous citywide. After a stroll in the streets, enjoy a plate or two, or sit with a beer on a seaside terrace or the *chiringuito*s (beach bars) scattered around the 1,100–metre sandy beach. A swim in the gorgeous water is also highly recommended during summer. The beach is equipped with shower and bathrooms.

"Have good rice at Kaiku (Pl. del Mar, 1). Bodega l'Electricitat (c/Sant Carles, 15) is another must."

– Atipus

12 Parc Güell
Map C, P.102

When Antoni Gaudí took up this project in 1900, it was intended as a private "garden city" with roughly 60 sea-facing houses. A Greek theatre and a hypostyle marketplace were to be provided among naturalistic decoration, but only two houses were eventually built. Gaudí later occupied the show home (now Gaudí House Museum), and enterpriser Eusebi Güell moved into the preexisting Casa Larrard which is now a school. Buy tickets in advance and arrive on the dot as visits to the Monumental zone are limited to 400 tickets and timed for half an hour from the reservation time.

🕐 0830-1815 (1 Jan-24 Mar, 28 Oct-31 Dec), -1900 (17 Feb-24 Mar), 0800-2130 (30 Apr-26 Aug), -2030 (25 Mar-29 Apr, 27 Aug-27 Oct) 💲 €8.50/6/Free for 6– 🏠 c/Olot, 5, la Salut, 08024 📞 +34 93 40 91 831 🔗 www.parkguell.cat

"At this location (av. Coll del Portell, 112) you will not find any tourists around."

– UnitedFakes

Cultural & Art Space

Art factories, multidisciplinary galleries and creative spaces

It is becoming increasingly harder to speak of disciplines or genres in Barcelona's cultural scene since the launch of its "Art Factories" programme. This initiative, run by the city and its Culture Institute, transforms disused spaces into new powerhouses of culture and knowledge to promote social involvement. The opening of independent galleries and art spaces fosters a healthy tendency towards artistic cross-disciplinarity, allowing a liberal platform for individual and unconventional expressions through dance and movement, theatre, circus, visual and sound arts. Independent galleries, private initiatives and bookshops also highlight Barcelona's creative spirit with comprehensive showcases and programmes in many disciplines, from architecture to spatial design. For regular cultural activities, spend time at Art Factories, Fabra i Coats (#16), as well as other centres like MACBA (#13), CCCB (#21), and Arts Santa Mònica (www.artssantamonica.cat). For local and international artist work, go to Hangar (#18), N2 Galería (#15) or Mutuo (#19). On Mount Montjuïc, visit Fundació Joan Miró (#14), MNAC (#22), CaixaForum Barcelona (#24) and the beautiful Botanic Garden in one trip.

Bernat Fortet Unanue
Multimedia designer

I worked in the entertainment industry in the past, but more recently focus on apps that change people life's in an impactful and meaningful way.

Fundació Joan Miró
036

Crajes
Artist duo

Carla and Jessica as one: Crajes. We have been working together since 2009. The best definition for our work so far is "girly grotesque."

Hey
Graphic design studio

We are a small studio based in Barcelona and mostly work on brand identity, illustration and editorial design, and with geometry, colour and direct typography.

MACBA
034

N2 Galería
037

GIF ME
Multimedia design studio

An interactive installation service, and investigation project led by Daniel Armengol Altayó. Our final goal is to set a creative stage for new interactive experiences.

Museu Marítim
040

Ivan Castro
Calligrapher

Working freelance on calligraphy, lettering and typography and also teaching in Elisava, BAU and Visions. I am also a tropical bartending geek.

Georgina Santiago
Fashion designer

Born and based in Barcelona. I studied fashion design and worked as a forecaster. My aim is to become a trend forecaster, be inspired and inspire others.

Fabra i Coats
038

Hangar
042

You are so Overrated
Art director & DJ

You are so Overrated is Chini. I'm a freelance art director, illustrator and DJ. You Are So Overrated is my personal project which includes illustrations, videos, comics and lots of other stuff!

Miscelänea
044

Chamo San
Artist

I'm an illustrator born and based in Barcelona. I graduated in Fine Arts at Universitat de Barcelona and spent a year at École Nationale Supérieure des Beaux-Arts in París.

Dvein
Multimedia studio

A collaborative project by directors Fernando Domínguez, Teo Guillem and Carlos Pardo providing direction and art direction for live action and animation.

Mutuo Centro de Arte
043

CCCB
045

Sergio Mora
Artist

I am an artist chameleon who lives in a spaceship landed on the artistic quarter of Poblenou. I am dedicated to painting, illustration, video, music, and performance.

Museu Frederic Marès
050

Nacho Alegre
Publisher, apartamento

Born and raised in Barcelona, I work as a photographer and publisher (apartamento magazine) and live with my girlfriend and my dog.

Lusesita
Artist

My name is Laura, but I work under the name of Lusesita. I'm from Rioja and have lived in Barcelona for ten years where I work on sculpture and ceramics.

MNAC
046

CaixaForum Barcelona
051

13 Museu d'Art Contemporani de Barcelona (MACBA)
Map E, P.107

Standing in marked contrast to its medieval locale, the white and unmistakably modern MACBA building is infused with late 20th century avant-garde attitude and El Raval's multicultural spirit. Every Saturday from 7pm live music and experimental art programmes take place next to its rolling exhibitions of contemporary art by Catalan and Spanish artists, North African and Eastern European art. The centre's substantial art book and catalogue archive is kept at MACBA Study Centre (*pl. dels Àngels 8, El Raval*), and is accessible with identification.

🕐 1100–1930 (M, W–F), 1000–2000 (Sa), –1500 (Su)
💲 €10/8/Free for 14–
🏠 pl. dels Àngels, 1, El Raval, 08001
📞 +34 93 48 13 368 URL www.macba.cat

"Awesome architecture and content. Enjoy one of the most popular skating spots (the square in front) in Europe, and nearby artistic and underground shops."
– Bernat Fortet Unanue

14 Fundació Joan Miró
Map G, P.109

Find the almost complete oeuvre of Joan Miró (1893-1983) on the slope of Montjuïc. Chiefly donated by Miró, over 14,000 pieces of abstract paintings, sculptures, textiles and ceramics reveal the itinerant artist's philosophies of art across the iconic building designed by Josep Lluís Sert (1902-83), Miró's lifelong friend. The museum also hosts a small contemporary art collection formed posthumously as a tribute. Expand the journey at Parc Joan Miró and Barcelona Airport Terminal B where more of his colossal pieces stand.

🕐 1000-1800 (T,W,F, Nov-Mar), -2000 (T,W,F, Apr-Oct & Sa), -2100 (Th), -1500 (Su)
💲 €12/7/5/2.50/Free for 15-
🏠 Parc de Montjuïc, Montjuïc, 08038
📞 +34 93 44 39 470
🔗 www.fundaciomiro-bcn.org

"It is a must see for Miró's lovers. And the building is wonderful."

– Hey

15 N2 Galería

Map D, P.104

Hiding away from Eixample's chaotic roads, the beautiful tree-lined Enric Granados street is graced with 20th-century architecture, broad walkways, outdoor cafés and reputable galleries. One of them is ground-floor gallery N2. Presenting eight exhibitions a year, mainly solo projects by young international artists, recent shows have presented Péjac, Crajes and Jorge Rodriguez Gerada, with installation, photography, video and fine art paintings. Enjoy art and the city on the street in equal amounts. Thursday evenings are chock-full with openings.

🕑 1100-1400, 1700-2030 (M-F) 🏠 c/Enric Granados, 61, L'Antiga Esquerra de l'Eixample, 08008 📞 +34 93 45 20 592
🔗 www.n2galeria.com

"It's a great gallery for the variety of artists they present. Each exhibition is a surprise."
– Crajes

16 Fabra i Coats
Map A, P.102

An icon of Barcelona's industrial heritage, the red-brick spinning mill built in the 1920s now houses cultural incubator Fabra i Coats, one of the ten 'Art Factories' initiated by the city's Culture Institute. Since 2008, the 6,500sqm space has been shared among art units, micro-enterprises and emerging artists who periodically stage performances fusing theatre, dance, music and visual arts. In between, exhibitions, cultural festivals and movie premieres take place. Look out for little art projects scattered through the floors. Other well-loved "Factories" include Hangar (*Emilia Coranty 16, el Poblenou*).

🕘 0900–2200 (M–F), 1000–2030 (Sa)
🏠 c/Sant Adrià, 20, Sant Andreu, 08030
☎ +34 93 25 66 150
🌐 fabraicoats.bcn.cat

"It's where I started my first project. Check the programme frequently as the activities change a lot from one day to another."
– GIF ME

17 Museu Marítim
Map E, P.107

With origins in the 14th century, this former royal shipyard, located at the waterfront of Ciutat Vella (Old Town district), now preserves Barcelona's naval history, with old maps, pictures, navigational instruments, test models and full size replica ships on permanent display. Boats of many different categories are represented, spanning medieval galleys, merchant ships, wooden submarine and racing boats dating back to the 1560s. The Gothic architecture, which will offer 10,000sqm of exhibition space after renovation, is due to fully reopen in late 2014. The project extends to Portal de Santa Madrona, the only remains of a medieval city old wall and gate at the fringe.

🕙 1000–2000 daily 💲 €5/4/2
🏠 av. de les Drassanes, el Raval, 08001 📞 +34 93 34 29 920
URL www.mmb.cat
📎 Free entry after 1500 (Su)

"The building itself is pretty impressive. Its permanent collection shows a lot of maritime culture and navigation history."
– Ivan Castro

18 Hangar
Map I, P.110

Artists looking for inspiration will find Hangar a unique hub of ideas and talent. Formally a centre for art research and production, it offers integral support to visual artists and creators along different phases of their projects in the form of equipment, imaging labs, co-working studios, and even a residential space. Located in a building originally designed for the textile industry in the mid-19th century, its backdrop is ideal for creative pursuits. Stop by for workshops or programmes organised by the resident artists and expand your horizons.

🕐 1000-1400, 1600-1930 (Mo-Fr)
🏠 Fundació AAVC Hangar, Emilia Coranty, 16,
08018 📞 +34 93 30 84 041
URL http://hangar.org

"Check the programme before going."
– Georgina Santiago

19 Mutuo Centro de Arte
Map F, P.108

A melting pot for Barcelona's vibrant art scene, this independent institution shows an amazing variety of artistic styles and voices. Independent producers, musicians and artists all appear in a weekly line-up, staged at the former garage, where the dim-lit, minimal interior is roughly divided between a mini-theatre, coffee lounge and art gallery and is accentuated with a mix of vintage leather chairs. Mutuo also sells designer goods ranging from jewellery, fashion, zines and art prints made by designers from around the world.

🕑 *Varies according to event*
🏠 *c/Méndez Núñez, 7, 08003*
📞 *+34 67 53 16 999* **URL** *http://mutuo.ca*

"The space and the exhibitions are some of the best in town."

– Chini aka You are so Overrated

20 Miscelänea

Map E, P.107

No better word than the name of this place could denote the assorted world of art enclosed in this artistic compound. With a gallery at the front and an "art laboratory" at the back, Miscelänea is a haven for things original and experimental shown in exhibitions, art markets, workshops and special events, curated in-house by a team of practising designers, illustrators and graphic artists. Creative brains set to work in the gallery's centre. They sell an interesting selection of independent publications, design objects and original prints selected from each show.

🕐 1700–2300 (W–Th, Su), –0000 (F–Sa)
🏠 c/Guardia, 10, el Raval, 08001
📞 +34 93 31 79 398
URL www.miscelanea.info

"The gallery is a showcase of young talents and artworks. The upstairs is where their cozy beautiful bar hides."
– Chamo San

21 Centre de Cultura Contemporània de Barcelona (CCCB) *Map E, P.107*

With a solid multidisciplinary programme, CCCB connects visitors with the city and urban culture day in, day out. Diverse exhibitions, parties, outdoor cinema, music festivals and performances all alternately enliven the 19th century workhouse and courtyard, where cultural gatherings are completed with a nice bookshop and a cool nine-to-nine bar. Five-day literature festival Kosmopolis celebrates the oral, printed and digital art of words with exhibitions, talks and songs.

🕐 1100-2000 (Tu-Su & P.H.)
💲 €8/6/4/Free for 12-
🏠 c/Montalegre, 5, el Raval, 08001
☎ +34 93 30 64 100
🔗 www.cccb.org

"Free admission every Sunday from 3-8pm!"

– Dvein

 22 Museu Nacional d'Art de Catalunya (MNAC)
Map G, P.109

Admire one of world's most extensive Romanesque art collections inside the grand National Palace, built for the 1929 International Exposition. Comprising murals, wood carvings, metalwork and stone sculptures in diverse styles, the collection forms a valuable mark of Catalan visual art movements, which extends to Gothic, Renaissance, Baroque and Modern art. Exhibits also include a rotating selection of 19th to 20th century photography, design and drawings by important Spanish artists like Marià Fortuny, Antoni Gaudí and Salvador Dalí. Still thirst for more? MNAC organises guided tours to its art reserves on Fridays at 4.30pm, and architecture reserve on Sundays at 11am. Booking required.

🕐 1000–1800 (Tu–Sa, Oct–Apr), –2000 (Tu–Sa, May–Sep) & –1500 (Su, P.H.) 💲 €14/12/2/Free for 16–
🏠 Palau Nacional, Parc de Montjuïc, 08038
📞 +34 93 62 20 360 🌐 www.mnac.cat

"If you want to relax a little, I recommend sitting on the stairs in front of MNAC and view Barcelona from Montjuïc."

– Sergio Mora

23 Museu Frederic Marès
Map E, P.107

Trained as a sculptor, notable for his post-civil war restoration work and monumental sculptures at Plaça de Catalunya, Frederic Marès (1893–1991) had also developed a love for collecting by the age of 18. Go straight up to the Collector's Cabinet to find thousands of 19th century objects, including clocks, pipes, weapons, cigar papers and toys that Marès used to stock in his study and donated to the city in 1944. The sculptor's own work and a sculpture collection are also exhibited in the medieval palace building, with a beautiful courtyard sitting next to Barcelona Cathedral.

🕐 1000–1900 (Tu–Sa), 1100–2000 (Su & P.H.)
💲 €4.20/2.40/Free for 16–　🏠 pl. de Sant Iu, 5–6, el Gòtic, 08002　📞 +34 93 25 63 500
🌐 www.museumares.bcn.cat
🖋 Free entry every 1st Su (1100–2000)

"It's a beautiful collector's museum that even locals haven't heard of."

– Nacho Alegre, apartamento

 24 **CaixaForum Barcelona**
Map G, P.109

Lovers of Art Nouveau architecture and contemporary art will enjoy CaixaForum's changing shows held at this former textile factory, built in 1911 by legendary architect and a contemporary of Gaudí and Domènech i Montaner, Josep Puig i Cadafalch (1867–1956). To enter its superior exhibition space, visitors first encounter a minimalist "secret garden" before descending an escalator under a steel and glass tree sculpture to an open white stone courtyard, which were all added by Japanese architect Arata Isozaki (b. 1931) between 1999–2002. Book junkies should not miss the forum's media library and Laie bookshop, which stocks an excellent array of novels as well as books on architecture, art and film.

🕐 *1000–2000 daily & P.H.*
🏠 *av. Francesc Ferrer i Guàrdia, 6–8,*
la Font de la Guatlla, 08038 📞 *+34 93 47 68 600*
🌐 *https://caixaforum.es*

"There are always interesting exhibitions alongside architecturally beautiful buildings."
– Lusesita

Markets & Shops

Handicrafts, design books and Catalan treats

Forget souvenirs on Ramblas. Instead, lose yourself in Catalan's designer shops, antique bazaars and centuries-old family businesses, many of whom are dedicated to producing original works. Friendly owners are happy to explain their selections or suggest products for your liking. Traditional groceries and food markets always guarantee a treasure hunt. If you're into handicrafts, Après Ski (#31) and the annual festival Festivalet (*www.festivalet.org*) by Duduà (*duduadudua.blogspot.com*) display handmade goods and accessories. Pay a visit to the designer-run Vostok Printing Shop (#30) too, for terrific silkscreen supplies, and Sabater Hermanos (#28) for handcrafted soaps. Those hungry for books, especially on art and design, should stop by La Central (*www.lacentral.com*) and Loring Art (*www.loring-art.com*), or Fatbottom (#32) for comics and art prints, while those hungry for delicious delicacies can satisfy cravings at Colmado Quílez (#35) or la Boquería (#36). Vila Viniteca (*www.vilaviniteca.es*) sells exceptional Catalan wines, with the best coming from Priorat or Montsant region. Take that, a blanket, a few candles and head down to Nova Icària or Bogatell beach to set yourself up a nice picnic dinner by the sea.

Cristobal Castilla
Director, Aer Studio

I'm a co-founder of Aer Studio, specialising in digital design for web and mobile services. I love food (specially brunch) and am a table-tennis addict.

Dosnoventa Urban Bikes 057

Christian Villacañas Camps, *Artist*

I usually spend the day drawing, reading comic books and graphic novels as well as writing. I'm also into learning about printing and bookbinding.

Marc Castellví Hernandez, *Filmmaker*

Born in Barcelona in 1989. I'm currently working freelance. I'm also involved in No más – de mamá, a gastronomic, graphic and audiovisual project.

Chandal 056

Laura Banchik
Fashion designer

I'm from Argentina and have lived in Barcelona since 2008. I design textiles and jewellery under the name of FARÖ. For me, Barcelona is a very inspiring place to live.

Lost & Found Market 058

Jazz Messengers 060

Oriol Malet
Founder, Malet & Co.

I am an illustrator and work with La Vanguardia newspaper, TimeoutBCN entertainment magazine, the cultural magazine Jot Down, etc and illustrated books of all kinds.

Slow
Graphic design studio

We are an independent creative team whose work goes from conceptualisation to execution, emphasising on the process and exploring the limits of each idea.

Sabater Hermanos 059

Vostok Printing Shop 061

Miju Lee
Illustrator

South Korean now settled in Barcelona. I draw, paint and make things with clay. It's a great pleasure for me to connect with people with what I'm doing and sharing my view of the world.

Fatbottom
063

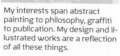

Antonio Ladrillo
Graphic designer

My interests span abstract painting to philosophy, graffiti to publication. My design and illustrated works are a reflection of all these things.

Lucía Vergara Ballester
Jewellery designer, Après Ski

I love what I do, and so I spend most of my time in the studio hand-lacquering and sanding pieces, while listening to music planning my next holiday/trip.

Après Ski
062

Oscar H.
Grand
064

Colmado
Quílez
066

Sergi Puyol
Illustrator

I've published three comic books with Apa–Apa Còmics and run the Colibrí Fanzine with Toni Mascaró from Apa–Apa. I'm also a drummer and composer for my bands.

Dorian
Graphic design studio

Founded in 2009 by Gaëlle Alemany and Gabriel Morales, Dorian is a small studio located in Barcelona specialising in corporate identity, packaging and editorial design.

David Espluga
Founder, espluga+associates

Creative director at espluga+associates. I love swimming, riding my bike and running. Love discovering new places to enjoy with people I love.

De Ubieta
065

Mercat de la
Boquería
067

25 Chandal
Map F, P.108

Retro camera lovers and collectors will lose heart and mind to this captivating store. Stocking an unbeatable concentration of toy cameras, vintage cameras, rare models and accessories and film for Polaroid and lomography, Chandal also offers a Super 8 film package that covers film development. (Normally the service takes three to four weeks.) Music is another strength. Unconventional offerings, mainly vinyls, highlight dynamic selections in electronic, experimental and pop. If you are in luck, you'll uncover exhibitions or artist meetings during your visit.

🕐 1100–1400, 1630–2100 (M-Sa)
🏠 c/Tantarantana, 16 & c/Allada Vermell, 13, 08003
☎ +34 93 31 83 819
URL shop.chandal.tv

"It also offers a great selection of vintage objects. Worth a visit when you are around the streets of CCCB (#21) and MACBA (#13)."

– Cristobal Castilla, Aer Studio

26 Dosnoventa Urban Bikes
Map C, P.105

Cycling has been big in Barcelona for a long
while now, and Dosnoventa Urban Bikes
has been at the forefront of the fixie scene
throughout the ebbs and flows of its popularity.
The brand was born out of the founders' dream
of making their own frames, and has been
turning the head of fixie fans from all over the
world ever since. Components are made in
Italy to the aesthetics, geometry, and image
crafted by the local team and sold in-store and
online. Go there for ideas and parts to build
your own custom bike with the help of the
friendly staff.

🕐 1530–1800 (Mo–Th), 1000–1500 (Fr)
🏠 Passatge de Bocabella, 5, 08013
📞 +34 93 66 75 154
URL shop.dosnoventabikes.com

*"If you're planning to buy a bike,
especially a fixie, this is your place."*

– Christian Villacañas Camps

27 Lost & Found Market
Map F, P.108 / Map H, P.110

If you have a penchant for pre-loved items and vintage treasures, the Lost & Found Market is a must-stop for stylish souvenirs and wardrobe additions. Bargain hunters will appreciate the colourful variety of stalls to explore, while discerning fashionistas are bound to come across statement pieces and a rare designer gem or two. With DJs playing alongside street food vendors and bars serving beer and vermouth, the vibes are fun and party-like. Details change with the seasons, so check online beforehand.

🕐 4 times a year over Sa & Su
🏠 Antiga Fàbrica Estrella Damm, c/Rossellò, 515, 08025
📞 +34 67 46 96 177
URL http://lostfoundmarket.com

"*If you are in Barcelona during Lost and Found Market edition you can't miss it.*"

– Marc Castellví Hernandez, No más – de mamá

28 Sabater Hermanos
Map E, P.107

Lose yourself in a world of aromatic wonders at Sabater Hermanos, where third generation soap makers offer their handmade creations in a variety of colours, shapes, and scents. While the soaps are made with a premium 100%-vegetable oil base, care was given to minimise damage to the environment in the process. The brand even does customisations for cosmetic lines, spas, and airlines. Drop by this charming boutique tucked away from the ever-busy Barri Gòtic to browse for a fun, fragrant gift like the 'fruit box', or beautiful floral bars with real petals as a personal treat.

🕙 1000–2000 (Mo–Sa), 1300–1900 (Su)
🏠 pl. Sant Felip Neri, 1, 18, 08002
☎ +34 93 30 19 832
URL www.shnos.com.ar

"Not only are the soaps great, but the whole store experience is worth a visit."
– Laura Banchik

29 Jazz Messengers
Map D, P.104

The name "Jazz Messengers" is a tribute to jazz giant Art Blakey and his hard-bop band and a note on the genre they specialised in. Over 15,000 records (CDs, LPs, and vinyl) and books present a comprehensive collection of international and Catalan labels, re-issues, hard-to-find albums and secondhand records showcasing gems in jazz classic, modern jazz, West Coast and Latin jazz, among others. Since 1980, the store has promised to supply "the best jazz at the best price." Their monthly catalogue details latest promotions and new arrivals to the store.

🕐 1030-1400, 1600-2030 (Tu-F), 1030-1430, 1630-2030 (Sa) 🏠 Córsega 202, Bajos-Derecha, L'Antiga Esquerra de l'Eixample, 08036
📞 +34 93 44 07 105 URL www.jazzmessengers.com

"For jazz lovers (like me)."
– Oriol Malet, Malet & Co.

30 Vostok Printing Shop

Map F, P.108

The ultimate playground for designers and craft enthusiasts, Vostok is stuffed with all sorts of first-class art supplies needed for silk screening, block printing, lettering and lithography. Inks, cutting tools, stencils and stamps are systematically categorised, alongside printing kits for various skill levels and materials for batik. If you are unsure what you need or how to transfer your thoughts into your prints, take advantage of the specialist staff. Practicing designer Alexis Rom occasionally runs workshops to demonstrate basic and unconventional stamping and engraving skills.

🕐 1000–1400, 1600–2000 (M–F), 1100–1430 (Sa)
🏠 C/Lluís el Piadós, 4, 08003
☎ +34 93 31 91 889
URL www.vostokshop.eu

"Go open-minded and let them tell you about new products."

– Slow

061

31 Après Ski
Map F, P.108

Everybody needs some statement jewellery as style go-tos, and Après Ski is the perfect place to find unique accessories that are timeless yet eye-catching. Designer Lucia Vergara uses antique materials from the 1940s to 1980s to create stunning pieces that are modern and casual, yet romantic at the same time. With themes that centre on flora, fauna, geometrics and the universe, pick up a brass necklace or scarf from her limited edition collections that seamlessly blend beautiful aesthetics and craftsmanship.

🕐 1100-1400, 1600-2000 (Mo-Sa)
🏠 c/Vigatans, 11, 08003
📞 +34 67 03 45 612
URL http://apresski.es

"If you are looking for some authentic Spanish design, I strongly recommend you to visit Après Ski's shop and look at her collection."
– Miju Lee

32 Fatbottom

Map E, P.107

Fatbottom has a nose for good fanzines and underground comics. Stocking an eclectic range of classics, including everything from comic strip collections and translated works to some of the weirdest sci-fi, sex comics and children's books published around the world, this young bookshop is a repertory of contemporary graphic novels for every taste and age. Besides illustrated books, also expect to discover music, art prints, posters and stationery not seen in mainstream outlets. Fatbottom even hosts small live concerts on occasions.

🕐 1000–1400, 1700–2030 (M-F), 1100–1500 (Sa)
🏠 c/Lluna, 10, el Raval, 08001 ☎ +34 93 17 98 957
URL fatbottombooks.com

"Try attend an opening of one of their shows. They have a very good selection and you can feel the passion for this kind of publications on the air."

– Antonio Ladrillo

33 Oscar H. Grand
Map F, P.108

While a well-tailored suit will never go out of style, there is no reason for the wardrobe staple to be boring. Stitching expert Oscar H. Grand is a stickler for details, and his eponymous clothing store is the base from which he creates high-quality garments with personalised touches for loyal customers, as well as those looking for something made to measure for a memorable occasion. If you have no time for a custom order, browse through his off-the-rack collection for chic and comfortable pieces made from imported fabrics.

🕐 1130-1430, 1630-2030 (Tu-Sa)
🏠 c/Barra de Ferro, 7, 08003
📞 +34 93 31 97 662
URL www.oscarhgrand.com

"Ask him what's happening in the city as he is always well informed on concerts and events."
– Lucía Vergara Ballester, Après Ski

34 De Ubieta

Map J, P.111

Set up to break the barriers between form, function, and art without promoting mass consumption, De Ubieta is a Barcelona-based footwear brand that has been growing a discerning fan base with its strong principles and well-crafted products that celebrate individuality. From start to finish, each shoe is brought to life using high-quality materials and sustainable processes that do little damage to the environment. Artisanal and meticulously designed, a pair will make for a stylish souvenir that has even preserved the planet.

By appointment only
c/Miquel Romeu, 101, 08907
www.deubieta.com

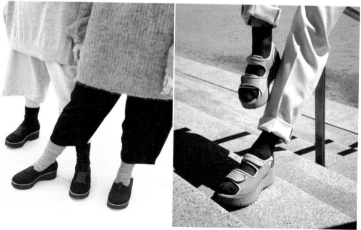

"Everything here is handmade with a stylish design and good prices."

– Sergi Puyol

35 Colmado Quílez
Map D, P.104

With floor-to-ceiling shelves chock-full of gourmet foods including liquors and wines, cured Ibérico hams, sausages, cheeses, teas, confectionary and preserves, this grocer's history shares its beginnings with the Palau de la Música Catalana, and began trading in 1908. Over 10,000 products are stocked, with a team of knowledgeable señores in blue smocks waiting to help you buy from your list. The LaFuente family, who owns the store and is known for its wineries, also sells their own cava Spanish sparkling wine and lines of products, from tinned foods to foie gras.

🕐 0900–1400, 1630–2030 (M–Sa)
📍 rbla. Catalunya, 65, Dreta de l'Eixample, 08007 📞 +34 93 20 11 513
URL www.lafuente.es

"Here you can buy the items for the most premium picnic ever."

– David Espluga, espluga+associates

36 Mercat de la Boquería
Map E, P.107

Any traveller should visit la Boquería at least once to discover Catalunya's passion for food. Its privileged location, together with gourmet offerings as varied as chocolate to fowl, seafood to innards, and amazing personalities at over 200 stalls and eateries prompt locals and tourists to wake up at the early hours to explore and enjoy the food. Among the many creatives who recommended la Boquería, one-third highlighted Bar Pinotxo for tapas. Go for jamón, cheese, olive oil and fruits here. Individual stores might close at 4pm from Monday to Thursday.

🕐 0800–2030 (M-Sa)
🏠 Rambla, 91, el Raval, 08001
☎ +34 93 31 82 584
URL www.boqueria.info

"The stands and bars closer to 'Las Ramblas' are more touristy and expensive than those near the back entrance."
– Dorian

Restaurants & Cafés

Gourmet tapas, seafood specialties and homemade vermouth

Barcelona has developed its age-old gastronomic theories alongside influences from Andalusian and Galician cuisine, and benefits from fresh local greens and fruits. Its coastal location adds an exquisite variety of fresh fish and shellfish, to inspire specialties like paella that are typically good in Barceloneta, the old fisherman quarter. Add to this good bread, cured sausages, calçots (scallion, plentiful in spring) and Catalan wine for a hint of the mouthwatering dishes on offer. Try the notable Tickets (*www.ticketsbar.es*) and Cal Pep (*www.calpep.com*) or, for a more casual dining, Bodega La Palma (#46) or Bar Bodega l'Electricitat (*c/Sant Carles 15, La Barceloneta*). La Pubilla (#38), little bars at el Mercat del Ninot (*www.mercatdelninot.com*) and la Boquería (#36) are also clever choices for tasty homemade food and real deal tapas. For innovative concepts, check out Pudding Bar (#42) and Fàbrica Moritz (#47), and on a Sunday morning follow the trend and quaff vermouth at Morro Fi (#52) and small nibbles before lunch at 2pm.

Bea Bascuñán
Graphic designer

I am in charge of Valencia-based studio Espacio Paco Bascuñán (EPB) and founder of independent publishing label, Publications for Pleasure. I also run a small screenprinting atelier.

Granja Petitbo
072

La Pubilla
073

Jordi Rins
Graphic designer

I'm currently working freelance with film production companies. I like designing film posters and promotional materials for movies.

Pablo Rovalo
Director, Research Studios

Trained as a visual designer in Mexico City and London, I live in Barcelona as a media professional with experience ranges from environmental graphics to motion graphics.

Bar El Velódromo
074

El Equipo Creativo
Interior design duo

Oliver Franz Schmidt and Natali Canas del Pozo began collaboration in 2010. The duo specialises in designing gastronomic spaces as well as brand and commercial projects.

Ikibana
076

La Cantina Palo Alto
077

Petz Scholtus
Founder, yök Casa + Cultura

I'm a no-stuff-designer, eco-creative and future hotelier from Luxembourg. My goal is to create a business for People, Planet and Profit that embraces the local culture in a fun and elegant way.

Bruno Sellés
Creative director, Vasava

Born in Barcelona, I am the founder of design studio Vasava, which develops solutions ranging from typography, illustration, interactive design to animation.

Pudding Bar
078

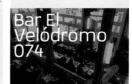

P·A·R
Graphic design studio

A graphic design and art direction studio based in Barcelona by Iris Tarraga and Lucía Castro.

Cuines Santa Caterina 080

Reskate Studio
Design studio

We are María López and Javier de Riba who create with sustainability in mind. Our work touches on graphic design, illustration, photography, video and installations.

Lyona
Filmmaker & illustrator

I started directing music videos for national and international bands after studying at ESCAC. I've published a children's book called "Yo mataré monstruos por ti" that is in its 7th edition.

Bodega Sepúlveda 079

Samsara 082

Mark Brooks
Graphic designer

I'm born here to a Catalan mother and an American father. I'm trained and worked as a designer in New York until 2010, and founded Mark Brooks Graphik Design in Barcelona.

Fàbrica Moritz 084

Tabula Rasa Studio
Graphic design studio

A young studio from Barcelona with graphic design base and experience in UX and UI. We develop projects ranging from corporate identity to web or apps design.

Laia Clos
Founder, Mot

I started my studio Mot in 2006 and now also teach at the Eina University (UAB). I am the vice president of the ADG FAD (Art Directors and Graphic Designers Association).

Bodega La Palma 083

Can Maño 085

37 **Granja Petitbo**
Map D, P.105

Large windows, high ceilings and sweet dec-
orations made from all sorts of bits and bobs
help make this charming corner café a local
hot spot for weekend brunch and peaceful
off-peak haven despite its location at the very
centre of Eixample. Fresh ingredients and pre-
cision cooking create unforgettable flavours
in well-presented simple dishes like crunchy
green salads, quinoa risotto, brie and smoked
salmon on toast topped with poached eggs,
and white chocolate pancakes. Granja Petitbo
is vegetarian-friendly and serves real coffee
at all hours.

🕐 0900–2300 (M–W), –0000 (Th,F), 1000– (Sa),
–2330 (Su)
📍 pg. Sant Joan, 82, Dreta de l'Eixample, 08009
📞 +34 93 26 56 503 🔗 www.granjapetitbo.com

*"Best to go during the week as the weekend and
especially brunch time gets quite busy. Juices and
cheesecake are highly recommended!"*

– Bea Bascuñán, Espacio Paco Bascuñán

38 La Pubilla
Map D, P.104

It is no surprise to find local cuisine at La Pubilla, as young owner and chef Alexis Peñalve draws his inspirations from Mercat de la Llibertat (Freedom Square), the farmers' market opposite. The trusty *menú del dia* at this neighbourhood cafe features tempting appetisers like pickled mushroom salad, cream of chickpea soup with olive sausage or mussels, followed by meat or seafood dishes and desserts for just €14. Every table receives complimentary bread and olives and a glass of wine, and vegetarian dishes can often be arranged on request.

🕐 0830-1700 (M), -0000 (Tu-F), 0900- (Sa) 🏠 pl. de la Llibertat, 23, Vila de Gràcia, 08012 📞 +34 93 21 82 994 f La Pubilla Gràcia

"This is where the best traditional and modern food of Barcelona can be found at a good price."

– Jordi Rins

39 **Bar El Velódromo**
Map D, P.104

Come here for the splendor of the art deco building at the upper end of carrer Muntaner and then stay for a palatable breakfast or choice of tapas. A popular meeting spot for politicians and artists in the mid-1900s, and later a nightclub, the establishment gained new life as a trendy cafe under the reins of Jordi Vilà, owner of Michelin-starred Alkimia (c/ Indústria 79, Vila de Gràcia). Make your way up the original staircase to the mezzanine floor to watch life downstairs. Standout dishes include *huevos estrellados* (fried eggs). The endearing menu design updates once a month.

🕐 0700-0300 (M-F), 0600- (Sa, Su)
🏠 c/Muntaner, 213, L'Antiga
Esquerra de l'Eixample, 08036
📞 +34 93 43 06 022

"Great retake on a classic Barcelona Bar."
– Pablo Rovalo, Research Studios

 Ikibana
Map E, P.106

From food philosophy to dazzling interior, Ikibana is a bright fusion of Japanese and Brazilian cultures. Cocktail bar, open kitchen and tables divide the place into several islands, and diners can watch mixologists shake drinks and chefs ornament plates with premium fish and tropical ingredients. Finish your gastronomic journey with a Sake Mojito, or "Cerveza," Ikibana's award-winning sweet course. Or dare yourself to try wasabi ice-cream.

🕐 1300–1400 (M–Th), –1500 (F–Su), –0100 daily for kitchen
🏠 av. del Paral-lel, 148, Sant Antoni, 08015 📞 +34 93 42 44 648
🔗 http://ikibana.com

 "A cool place for dinner and cocktails in Paralelo avenue, the theatre avenue in Barcelona."
– El Equipo Creativo

41 La Cantina Palo Alto

Map I, P.110

Less than ten minutes walk away from Metro station Selva de Mar (L4) stands Javier Mariscal's plant-covered fortress, Palo Alto. Buried among the lush mixed vegetation are the offices of some 20 creative units, outdoor meeting rooms, a kitchen garden and a staff bar that welcomes the public during office hours. La Cantina is a popular lunch place amongst creatives where Mediterranean cuisine is prepared with locally-sourced ingredients. Mariscal is also the creator of 1992 Barcelona Olympics' mascot, Cobi, and Oscar-nominated animated film *Chico & Rita* (2010).

🕐 1300-1530 (M-F)
🏠 Fundació Palo Alto, c/Pellaires, 30-38, 08019   ☎ +34 67 12 30 545
URL http://www.paloaltobcn.org

"Friday is paella day and if you're lucky you might spot Javier Mariscal himself!"

– Petz Scholtus, yök Casa + Cultura

 Pudding Bar
Map D, P.105

Kids and kids-at-heart will fall in love with the magical Alice in Wonderland-esque ambience at Pudding Bar, where gigantic mushrooms and a fantastical setting welcome diners into a fairy tale brought to life. Besides the delightful décor, there are board games and books to complement its delicious breakfast, cakes and pastries -making it a lovely place to keep the little ones busy and while the afternoon away. Wizard fans will also love its sister restaurant, Pudding Coffee House, which pays tribute to all things Harry Potter. Look out for family-friendly themed events, like chess matches on Tuesdays.

🕐 0900–2100 (Su–Fr), –2200 (Sa)
🏠 c/Pau Claris, 90, 08010
☎ +34 93 44 19 672
URL www.puddingbarcelona.com

 "If you're traveling with kids this is a must see place. Its gorgeous interior design will mesmerise the kiddos (and some adults too!)."
– Bruno Sellés. Vasava

43 Bodega Sepúlveda
Map E, P.106

If you are looking to enjoy traditional fare made with high-quality ingredients amidst an authentic bodega setting, this family-owned restaurant should be an essential pit stop in your Spanish culinary journey. Although it may seem like there are plenty of other places like it, Bodega Sepúlveda offers a leisurely local dining experience with excellent tapas, embutidos, and cooked specialties personalised by the chef amidst intimate interiors. Founded years ago as a wine house, it provides a foolproof setting for cosy cava-filled conversations.

🕐 1330–1630 (M–F), 2000–0100 (M–Sa)
🏠 c/Sepúlveda, 173, 08011
📞 +34 93 32 35 944 / +34 93 45 47 094
🔗 www.bodegasepulveda.net

"Don't forget to taste the scrambled trumpets and squid, it's really delicious!"

– P·A·R

44 Cuines Santa Caterina
Map F, P.108

A direct way to experience and gain inspiration from the fresh greens, fish and meat offered at Market Santa Caterina is to eat at their kitchen and tapas bar. Dishes like *botifarra*, grilled provolone cheese, Thai curry, tempura vegetables – are created using ingredients spotted under the colourful mosaicked canopy, cooked in Mediterranean, Asian or Spanish kitchens, and washed down with a good wine or freshly-pressed juices. Market Santa Caterina is a marketplace for all things grown in the area. One or two stalls are dedicated to Jabugo Ibérico ham.

🕐 1300–1600 (M–F), –1630 (Sa–Su), 1930–2300 (Su–Th), –2330 (Fr, Sa), Bar: 0900–2300 (Su–Th), –2330 (Fr, Sa) 🏠 av. Francesc Cambó, 16, Sant Pere, Santa Caterina i la Ribera, 08003 📞 +34 93 26 89 918 🔗 https://grupotragaluz.com/restaurante/cuines-santa-caterina

"The bar is where you can ask for a quick but delicious tapas and the restaurant for seasonal dishes with market products that are cooked in sight."

– Reskate Studio

45 Samsara

Map D, P.104

Samsara is more than just about its novel culinary creations. While the food is undoubtedly delicious with an eclectic mix of tapas influenced by flavours from all over the world, its cheerful North African décor fits right in with the laidback, bohemian spirit of the Gracia area – offering diners a casual atmosphere to relax in. Plates are ideal for sharing, with plenty of exciting options for vegetarians and coeliacs. For a more upbeat experience, head over on a weekend for the chance to enjoy your meal to music by a live DJ.

🕐 2030–0100 (M-T), 1930– (F-Su),
1300–1600 (Sa, Su)
🏠 c/Terol, 6, 08012
📞 +34 93 28 53 688
URL www.samsarabcn.com

"You can't go to Barcelona without trying the bravas served at Samsara, they're updated and surprising."

– Lyona

46 Bodega La Palma
Map F, P.108

Hidden in one of the historic Gothic Quarter's narrow streets, this wine house boasts more than 75 years of history, but remains young at heart. Try a true Catalan meal or authentic tapas (especially omelettes) served by warm, friendly staff in this unfussy traditional bodega (wine cellar) setting. The barman has encyclopedia-like knowledge on whiskies and other spirits. Let yourself be advised. Raw artisanal cheeses are some of the best you'll taste.

🕐 0900–0000 (M–F), 1200– (Sa)
🏠 c/Palma de Sant Just, 7, el Gòtic, 08002 📞 +34 93 31 50 656
URL www.bodegalapalma.com

"Best if you go on a week day. Take the L4 (yellow) subway to Jaume I and beware of the pickpockets."

– Mark Brooks, Mark Brooks Graphik Design

47 Fàbrica Moritz
Map E, P.106

Fàbrica Moritz, the first beer factory in Barcelona and benchmark of Catalan beer since 1856, is now a hip gastronomic destination where you can taste fresh, unpasteurized beer poured straight from the barrels at the microbrewery. Masterfully revived by starchitect Jean Nouvel, the 19th century building is separated into five zones, where you can revel in finger-licking tapas or brunch next to a vertical garden, buy signature Nouvel-designed Moritz chairs or partake in varying events held in underground fermentation halls. Go with time to spare if you plan on trying the factory route.

🕐 0900-0230 (M-F), -0300 (Sa, Su)
🏠 rda. Sant Antoni, 41, Sant Antoni, 08011   📞 +34 93 42 60 050
URL https://moritz.com/ca/fabrica-moritz

"There are interesting events every week. Check their facebook page and you'll surely find something to raise your interest."
– Tabula Rasa Studio

48 Can Maño
Map H, P.110

Everything from the hexagonal tiles and framed yellowed reviews, to the ceiling fans and handwritten bills, as well as the lovable father-owner informs this little tavern's long history of homestyle cooking. Fish, prawn (*gamba*) and squid fried or grilled with garlic and parsley continues to win over locals in the old fishermen's quarter, with tables highly sought even in the hottest months. Can Maño is very small and serves dinner only during the week. Arrive early as queues form way before opening time at 8pm.

🕐 0815–1100, 1215–1600, 2000–2300 (Tu–Sa), 2000–2300 (M)
🏠 c/Baluard 12, La Barceloneta, 08003
📞 +34 93 31 93 082

"*Normally filled by locals, it's a very good place to taste fresh and grilled seafood at very good prices. A really authentic and vivid place.*"

– Laia Clos, Mot

Nightlife

Live bands, cocktail classics and thematic concerts

Wherever you go at night in Barcelona, good music follows you around. Get sweaty dancing to DJ-spun disco and pop, and then wallow in an eclectic mix of jazz, roots, reggae, soul, techno, flamenco, caplo, funk or fusion at Heliogàbal (#56) or head to Sala Apolo (#57) for live shows and musician-run taprooms like Bar Vinil (#50) for more select playlists. Hit things off on a high note -- pick a high ground and view Barcelona's spectacular sunset, be it at Tibidabo, Bunkers del Carmel (#4), or Mount Montjuïc. Arrive around 7.30pm in summer or 3.30pm in winter to watch the city fade into the dusky pink light. After, sip cocktails that carry a taste of the 1950s at Boadas Cocktails (#53), watch a play in a 135 year-old location (#54), feel the energy of traditional Spanish Copla tunes at O'Barquiño (#59), or hit any of the terraces in Gràcia (if you're into beer, give Voll-Damm a shot). Summer travellers should hit up the great indie and electronic bands that appear at Primavera Sound (*www.primaverasound.com, May/June*).

Amaia Arrazola
Artist

Born in Basque, I studied advertising in Madrid and work in Barcelona. I like everything that has to do with illustration.

Bar Vinil
091

Paula Bonet
Artist

Based in Barcelona since 2012, I paint and draw for magazines, editorials, private commissions and also do mural paintings.

Pau Alekumsalaam
Graphic designer

Professional whistler and loser of valuable objects, student of all, almost guitarist for a day, writer without orthographic manual, compulsive winner and eternal aspirant to intellectual.

Cal Brut
090

La Cervecita
092

Querida
Graphic design studio

We are a design and communication studio based in Barcelona.

Boadas
Cocktails
094

Óscar Germade
Creative director, Solo

Creative director of an independent graphic design studio in Barcelona working on identity, editorial and packaging design.

Pietari Posti
Founder, Studio Posti

I'm a Finnish illustrator and graphic designer enjoying life in Barcelona. I get a kick from everything visual, from Belgium comics to modern furniture design.

Morro Fi
093

Bar de l'Antic
Teatre
095

clase bcn
Graphic design studio

A Barcelona-based studio made up of ten young multidiscipli-nary professionals who work on all areas of design, but pay particular attention to typeface and the element of surprise.

Heliogàbal
097

BET
Fashion design studio

Barcelona Experimentació Tèxtil (BET) is a project created by three designers in Barcelona driven by the need to experi-ence the many lives and possi-bilities of textile language.

Physalia
Multimedia design studio

Founded in 2007 in Barcelona, we work on 3D animation, pho-tography, live action, stop-mo-tion, robotics, electronics, etc. To us, every new project is a unique work of craftsmanship.

Ocaña
096

Sala Apolo
098

O'Barquiño
100

David Melgarejo Vicente
Journalist

I am a journalist and art and fashion creative. Urban culture and video art are two of my biggest obessions. Open your eyes because there are a lot of interesting stories surrounding you. You just have to find it!!

Cristina Spanò
Illustrator

I work primarily on editorial and comics, and projects with the collective Teiera. I look for ironic and direct ideas in my work.

Soledad Arismendi
Web designer

I'm director of "This is not a Company," with a passion for beauty in all its glory. My love for modern technologies has assisted me in setting up a plat-form for artists: WeArt Festival.

Cèntric
Canalla
099

JazzSí Club
101

49 **Cal Brut**
Map F, P.108

A reggae bar with true reggae soul. Called
"Dirty House," this hangout is brimming with
retro posters, Minorcan gin bottles, absurd
signs, characterful knick-knacks and Caribbean
music. Bob Marley overlooks a kitchenette,
where the barmen flip dishes as well as glasses
to prepare hearty tapa dishes made to match
drink of the moment, homemade vermouth.
Naturally, Cal Brut also carries Minorcan gin
and a selection of Spanish and imported beers
(from Jamaica, Belgium, Czech, the Nether-
lands, Germany).

🕐 1900-0100 (Su-W), -0200 (Th-Sa)
🏠 c/Princesa, 42, Sant Pere, Santa Caterina i la
Ribera, 08003 📞 +34 93 55 43 995
🔗 www.calbrut.cat

*"Not many bars in Born have barmen who can
remember you and your drink after your first visit.
A very, very friendly place to spend the night."*
– Amaia Arrazola

50 Bar Vinil

Map D, P.104

No attempt is made to create a bohemian night spot. Owner and guitarist with local band Inspira, Jordi Lanuza's carefully crafted playlist comprises such variation as classic rock, trip hop, jazz and twee pop, that turns this bar into an intimate spot dedicated to vinyl. Beside crowds of friendly locals, great musicians of the Catalan music scene are often seen holding a beer at the bar. Plaça de la Vila, the mythical neighbourhood square, is just around the corner, an added bonus.

🕐 2000–0230 daily
🏠 c/Matilde 2, Vila de Gràcia, 08012
📞 +34 66 91 77 945   ⓕ Bar Vinil

"Good music, nice people and great location. The owner, Jordi Lanuza is a really friendly guy that will receive you with a big smile."

– Paula Bonet

51 La Cervecita
Map I, P.110

Both an emporium and tasting room, La Cervecita Nuestra de Cada Dia is a beer-lover's paradise where over 200 obscure craft beers and imports can be sampled and purchased. American Flying Dog (porter), Scottish Brewdog (imperial stout) and Catalan lagers, are among selections that won over the hearts of owners Angie Gesteira and Joaquín Jané, but they can be fickle – the selection, served by the bottle with some on tap, constantly evolves and expands. At times, the couple also produces their own specialty brews for celebrations, such as the shop's November anniversary.

🕐 1130–1400 (W–Sa), 1730–2230 (M–Sa), –2130 (Su)
🏠 C/Llull, 184, el Poblenou 08005
📞 +34 93 48 69 271   ⓕ La Cervecita nuestra de cada dia

"It's like home to rest. Come in a lazy evening on a weekday and enjoy the calm of the local people. They have over 100 varieties of beers, and cheap! Halleluja!"
– Pau Alekumsalaam

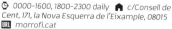

52 Morro Fi
Map E, P.106

From food blog to bar, Morro Fi seems to know well what can make life better. To get a good idea, ask for Marcel's "*vermut preparat*," Morro Fi's housemade vermouth (in Morro Fi-designed bottles, no less). The drink is recommended alongside extra thick crisps and other typical faves – canned mussels, cured anchovy fillets and crunchy green olives considered more "*aperitiu* (appetisers)" than tapas. Although a popular place for a drink after-hours, the hipster ritual in Barcelona is to sip vermouth just before Sunday lunch. To get in on the trend, make sure your Saturday night doesn't blot your Sunday morning.

⏱ 0000–1600, 1800–2300 daily 🏠 c/Consell de Cent, 171, la Nova Esquerra de l'Eixample, 08015
🔗 morrofi.cat

"*Another 'best' vermouth place with the best spicy chips, best vermouth, best beer, best people, and best waiter in town.*"

– Querida

53 Boadas Cocktails

Map E, P.107

Framed reportage prints, wooden stools and, more importantly, champion cocktails – good old tradition is well-kept in this mahogany-filled bar. Possibly the oldest barroom in town, opened by Havana-inspired mixologist Miguel Boadas in 1933, Boadas shakes a dry martini famous citywide and daiquiris that have lured esteemed clients like poet Sagarra and Nobel-prize winning playwright Jacinto Benavente. Joan Miró even has a concoction dedicated to him. The bar hasn't rested on its laurels – if you're up for something new, let the sleek-headed professionals on staff surprise you.

🕐 1200–0200 (M–Th), –0300 (F–Sa) 🏠 c/Tallers, 1, Vallvidrera, el Tibidabo i les Planes, 08001
📞 +34 93 31 89 592 URL boadascocktails.com

"Ask for an 'Old-Fashioned', nowhere is it better than in this place."

– Óscar Germade, Solo

54 Bar de l'Antic Teatre

Map E, P.107

Despite a central location, this little theatre can be hard to find. Don't let it fool you – it's not to be missed. Establishing itself as an independent space for contemporary performance art, Antic Teatre runs an eclectic programme, from circus to concerts and dance that deals with society, culture, politics and contemporary thought. The inner terrace and courtyard displays anarchic vegetation but is an oddly charming place where anyone can come anytime to slug back a beer. To enter, look for a small door in the middle of a dark alley south of Palau de la Música.

🕐 1000–2330 (M-Th), –1600 (F), 1700–0000 (Sa), –2200 (Su) 🏠 c/Verdaguer i Callís, 12, Sant Pere, Santa Caterina i la Ribera, 08003
📞 +34 93 31 52 354 URL www.anticteatre.com

"Escape the chaotic city to Antic Teatre's big courtyard terrace. At night it can get quite full and noisy but the drink prices are cheap."

– Pietari Posti, Studio Posti

 Ocaña
Map E, P.107

With enticing outdoor terrace facing the beautiful Plaça Reial, a chic café, the intriguing Apotheke cocktail bar, and a high-ceilinged restaurant connected to a club, Ocaña understandably seduces. Designer chairs, vintage fixtures and original pillars with oak flooring harmoniously blend within this fabulous building, a restoration by Albert Guilleumas and Mireia Campa, which took eight years to complete. Chat over a chilled frothy beer or a fancy cocktail, sample modern Catalan cuisine, and then dance under the DJ's gaze till the wee hours.

🕐 1700–0200 (M–F), 1500–0230 (Sa, Su & P.H.)
🏠 pl. Reial, 13–15, el Gòtic, 08002
📞 +34 93 67 64 814 URL www.ocana.cat

"It's real fun with a mixed crowd. Take care in the surrounding area though."

– clase bcn

56 Heliogàbal

Map D, P.104

Besides being a teeny little bar, Heliogàbal is a multidisciplinary platform for emerging talent and an unmissable stop for indie bands touring Barcelona. Their cultural offering is diverse. Several nights a week you can enjoy poetry readings, experimental music and live jazz concerts followed by open jam sections in this compact space. Photography exhibitions, magazine launches, audiovisual screenings and much more also take place. As a well known spot in the neighbourhood it fills up quickly.

🕐 2100 til late daily
🏠 c/Ramón y Cajal, 80, Vila de Gràcia, 08012 ☎ +34 93 67 63 132
URL www.heliogabal.com

"Arrive a little before 9pm, opening time. Do not miss the atmosphere at the entrance in between concerts. Sometimes the best parts happen outside."

– BET

57 Sala Apolo
Map E, P.107

Cutting-edge gigs and wild parties are non-stop at this top-ranked concert hall and club. Visiting and homegrown bands occupy main venue Sala Apolo and annexe La [2] de Apolo in the early evening, with musical styles ranging from techno through to reggae and swing. Indie rock and pop leads the way on "Nasty Mondays". Refined-pop lovers should also look out for "Old Wave New Wave" hosted by Miqui Puig every month. At midnight, the music halls morph into crazy club houses. Dance hard into the small hours every night except Sunday.

🕐 💲 Showtime & ticket price vary with programmes 🏠 c/Nou de la Rambla, 113, el Poble-sec, 08004 ☎ +34 93 44 14 001 URL www.sala-apolo.com

"Get ready to party. The best DJ's coming on Fridays."
– Physalia

58 Cèntric Canalla

Map E, P.107

Friendly and convivial, Cèntric Canalla has a classy interior mostly inherited from original occupant, Cèntric Bar, which first opened in 1941. Local interior designer Pilar Libano has given it a fantastic facelift, turning the place into a chic, retro café-bar now best known for their gin and tonics. Offered are more than 30 gins for pairings of your choosing. The kitchen serves excellent grub too, from hearty tapas plates to larger selections like burgers and omelette, as well as homemade pies. Head to the room at the back if you want to sit and eat with a group of friends.

🕐 0800–0100 (M–Th), –0200 (F),
0900–0200 (Sa), –0100 (Su)
🏠 c/Ramelleres, 27, el Raval, 08001
📞 +34 93 16 00 526
🔗 http://centricbar.com/es

"Gintonics!!"
– David Melgarejo Vicente

59 O'Barquiño
Map E, P.106

O'Barquiño is perhaps one of the best-kept secrets in el Raval. On first sight, it appears to be just another local restaurant, but go there on a Friday or Saturday night, ascend to the second floor and find yourself entering an alternate dimension: singers in drag living it up celebrating traditional Spanish song and copla. An appreciative audience often takes a break from plates of ham and glasses of wine to give an enthusiastic clap. Anyone free of prejudice is welcomed.

🕐 0900-0000 daily
🏠 c/Príncep de Viana, 1, el Raval, 08001
📞 +34 93 32 93 097
📘 O Barquiño Barcelona

"*Search 'O'Barquiño' in YouTube and you'll understand.*"

– Cristina Spanò

60 JazzSí Club

Map E, P.106

Live music fills this club every day and night. With a pedigree of over 35 years, JazzSí is part of Taller de Músics' (Musicians' Workshop) initiative to support young musicians. For a full-on journey of music, start with tributes to great jazz maestros every Monday, Cuban on Thursday, rock on Sunday and jazz or blues the rest of the time. Friday's flamenco nights are a real highlight, and start from 8.45pm. Other opening times vary from 6.30pm to 8.30pm. Admission includes first drink.

🕐 💲 *Showtime & ticket price vary with programmes* 🏠 *c/Requesens, 2, el Raval, 08001*
📞 *+34 93 32 90 020*
URL *tallerdemusics.com/jazzsi-club*

"It's a small and cosy live jazz club. On Fridays it hosts flamenco nights, and it's the best flamenco you can find in Barcelona, for real."

– Soledad Arismendi

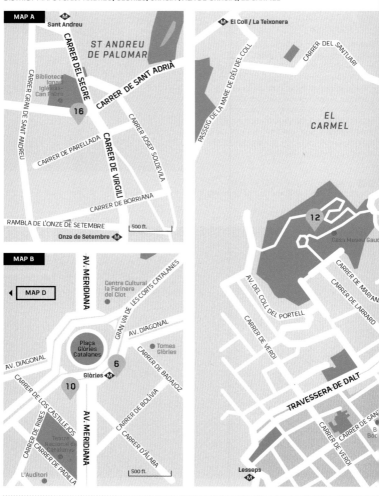

- 6_ Disseny Hub Barcelona
- 16_Fabra i Coats
- 10_Els Encants Vells
- 12_Parc Güell

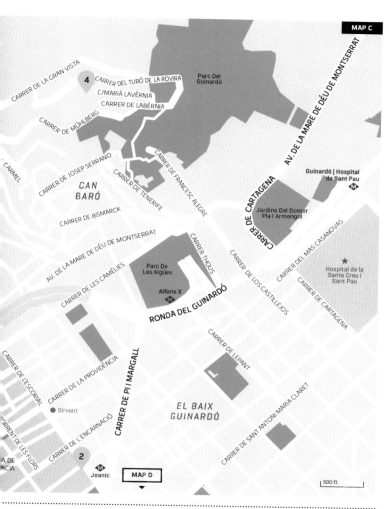

MAP C

CARRER DE LA GRAN VISTA

4 CARRER DEL TURÓ DE LA ROVIRA

Parc Del Guinardó

C/MARIÀ LAVÈRNIA

CARRER DE LABÈRNIA

CARRER DE MÜHLBERG

CARMEL

CARRER DE JOSEP SERRANO

AV. DE LA MARE DE DÉU DE MONTSERRAT

CAN BARÓ

CARRER DE TENERIFE

CARRER DE FRANCESC ALEGRE

CARRER DE BISMARCK

Guinardó | Hospital de Sant Pau Ⓜ

CARRER DE CARTAGENA

Jardins Del Doctor Pla I Armengol

AV. DE LA MARE DE DÉU DE MONTSERRAT

CARRER DE LES CAMÈLIES

Parc De Les Aigües

CARRER THOUS

CARRER DEL MAS CASANOVAS

★ Hospital de la Santa Creu i Sant Pau

CARRER DE LOS CASTILLEJOS

CARRER DE CARTAGENA

Alfons X Ⓜ

RONDA DEL GUINARDÓ

CARRER DE PI I MARGALL

CARRER DE LEPANT

CARRER DE L'ESCORIAL

CARRER DE LA PROVIDÈNCIA

Sirvent

CARRER DE L'ENCARNACIÓ

EL BAIX GUINARDÓ

CARRER DE SANT ANTONI MARIA CLARET

RRENT DE LES FLORS

A DE CIA

2

Joanic Ⓜ

MAP D ▼

500 ft.

- 2_Vila de Gràcia
- 4_Bunkers del Carmel

★ Modernista building

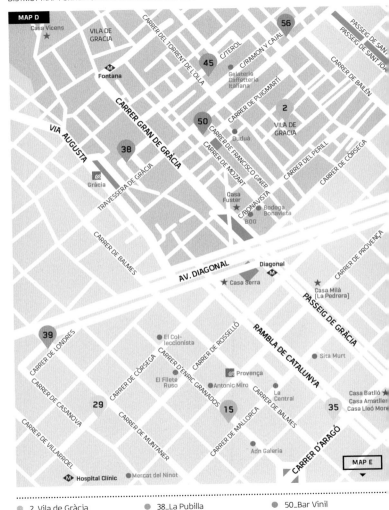

MAP C

Sagrada Família Ⓜ 9

CARRER DE CÒRSEGA

CARRER DE SICÍLIA

CARRER DE PROVENÇA

Plaça De La Sagrada Família

CARRER DE SARDENYA

CARRER DE LA MARINA

AV. DIAGONAL

Ⓜ Verdaguer

Monumental Ⓜ

● Plaça De Brans de la Monumental

AV. DIAGONAL

CARRER D'ARAGÓ

RETA DE EIXAMPLE

37

PASSEIG DE SANT JOAN

26

GRAN VIA DE LES CORTS CATALANES

CARRER DE GIRONA

CARRER DE ROGER DE FLOR

CARRER D'ARAGÓ

CARRER DE BAILÈN

RRER D'ARAGÓ

CARRER DEL CONSELL DE CENT

Ⓜ Girona

Ⓜ Tetuan

CARRER DE BAILÈN

CARRER DE GIRONA

CARRER D'ALÍ BEI

Ⓜ Ⓡ Arc de Triomf

GRAN VIA DE LES CORTS CATALANES

CARRER DEL BRUC

● Freaks Books

RONDA DE SANT PERE

de Triomf

E GRÀCIA

42

CARRER D'AUSIÀS MARC

★ Fundació Vila Casas

SANT PERE SANTA CATERINA I LA RIBERA

asseig de Gràcia

Ⓜ Ⓡ

Ⓜ Vraninaoua

500 ft.

· ·

● 9_La Sagrada Família
● 26_Dosnoventa Urban Bikes
● 37_Granja Petitbo
● 42_Pudding Bar

★ Modernista building

- 13_MACBA
- 17_Museu Marítim
- 20_Miscelänea
- 21_CCCB
- 23_Museu Frederic Marès
- 28_Sabater Hermanos
- 32_Fatbottom
- 36_Mercat de la Boquería
- 40_Ikibana
- 43_Bodega Sepúlveda
- 46_Bodega La Palma
- 47_Fàbrica Moritz

MAP D

RONDA DE SANT PERE

Ⓜ Urquinaona

Palau de la Música Catalana

54

PLAÇA DE CATALUNYA

DE BALMES

AV. PORTAL DE L'ÀNGEL

CARRER COMTAL

CARRER DE SANT PERE MÉS BAIX

Pl. Catalunya Ⓜ ✍ Ⓡ

CARRER DE PELAI

VIA LAIETANA

MAP F ▶

R DELS TALLERS

58

53

C/ LES RAMELLERES

LA RAMBLA

LA RAMBLA

23

La Central del MUHBA

Ⓜ Jaume I

CARRER DELS ÀNGELS

21

àngels barcelona

Cathedral de Barcelona

13

Orolíquido

Satan's Coffee Corner

28

Palau de la Generalitat

46

JOAQUÍN COSTA

CARRER DEL PEU DE LA CREU

CARRER DEL CARME

36

EL BARRI GÒTIC

32

LA LLUNA

Ⓜ Liceu

CARRER DE FERRAN

La Manual Alpargatera

E LA RIERA ALTA

LA RAMBLA

CARRER D'AVINYÓ

R DE SANT ANTONI ABAT

CARRER DE L'HOSPITAL

55

CARRER DE SANT PAU

Jamboree Jazz

CARRER AMPLE

EL RAVAL

CARRER DE SANT PAU

CARRER NOU DE LA RAMBLA

★ Güell Palace

20

LA RAMBLA

LA RAMBLA

AV. DE LES DRASSANES

Arts Santa Monica

PASSEIG DE COLOM

Drassanes

17

Ⓜ Paral·lel

57

AV. DEL PARAL·LEL

CARRER DE VILA I VILÀ

DÀRSENA NACIONAL

500 ft.

· ·

● 52_Morro Fi
● 53_Boadas Cocktails
● 54_Bar de l'Antic Teatre
● 55_Ocaña

● 57_Sala Apolo
● 58_Cèntric Canalla
● 59_O'Barquiño
● 60_JazzSí Club

★ Modernista building

107

DISTRICT MAP : **CIUTAT VELLA (EL GÒTIC, LA RIBERA, EL BORN), SANT MARTÍ (VILA OLÍMPICA)**

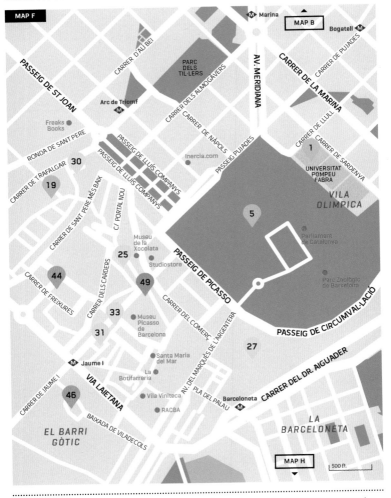

- 1_Dipòsit de les Aigües
- 5_Parc de la Ciutadella
- 19_Mutuo Centro de Arte
- 25_Chandal
- 27_Lost & Found Market
- 30_Vostok Printing Shop
- 31_Après Ski
- 33_Oscar H. Grand
- 44_Cuines Santa Caterina
- 46_Bodega La Palma
- 49_Cal Brut

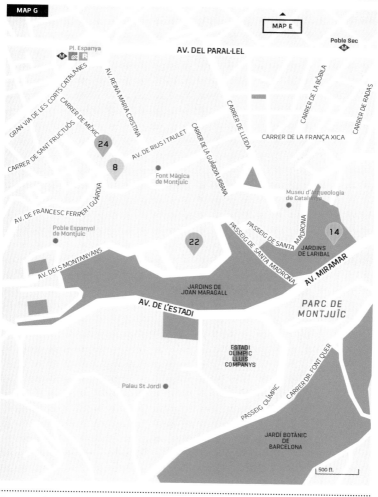

- 8_Pavelló Mies van der Rohe
- 14_Fundació Joan Miró
- 22_MNAC
- 24_CaixaForum Barcelona

DISTRICT MAPS : **LA BARCELONETA, SANT MARTÍ (EL POBLENOU)**

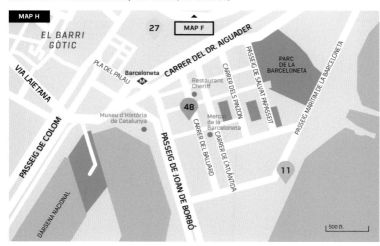

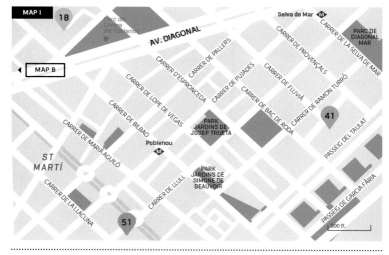

- ● 11_La Barceloneta
- ● 18_Hangar
- ● 27_Lost & Found Market
- ● 41_La Cantina Palo Alto
- ● 48_Can Maño
- ● 51_La Cervecita

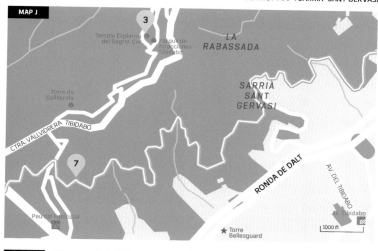

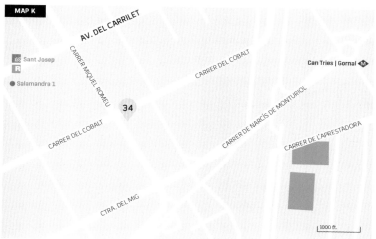

- 3_Tibidabo (Eixample)
- 7_Carretera de les Aigües
- 34_De Ubieta

★ *Modernista building*

Accommodation

Hip hostels, fully-equipped apartments & swanky hotels

No journey is perfect without a good night's sleep to recharge. Whether you're backpacking or on a business trip, our picks combine top quality and convenience, whatever your budget.

 <€80    €81–200   €201+

DestinationBCN

Comfort and style co-exist here. Twenty one- and two-bedroom pied-à-terre suites (45–120 sqm) share spectacular views of Eixample. Going upscale? Try the penthouse suite with private terrace. Guests can ask for anti-allergic pillows if necessary.

🏠 rda. Universitat, 11, Dreta de l'Eixample, 08007
📞 +34 93 53 25 267
🔗 www.destinationbcn.com

El Palauet

Palauet is Catalan for "small palace," and so this is. The five-storey modernist mansion, built by Pere Falqués in 1906, houses six apartment-suites, where historic settings are partnered with modern furnishings and technology. Each suite is taken care of by a personal assistant, who can assist on meals and shopping needs.

 pg. Gràcia, 113, Vila de Gràcia, 08008
+34 93 218 0050 URL www.elpalauet.com

Generator Hostel Barcelona

Generator is reputed to provide economy lodgings with flair. Its new Barcelona flagship goes better by adding private terraces to twin en-suite rooms. The hostel is just a ten-minute walk away from main metro stations, Diagonal and Verdaguer. Reception opens 24 hours.

🏠 c/Còrsega, 373, Vila de Gràcia, 08037
📞 +34 93 22 00 377
URL www.generatorhostels.com

Casa Camper Barcelona

🏠 c/Elisabets, 11, El Raval, 08001
📞 +34 93 34 26 280
URL www.casacamper.com

Grand Hotel Central

🏠 Vía Laietana, 30, la Ribera, 08003
📞 +34 93 29 57 900
URL www.grandhotelcentral.com

Hotel OMM

🏠 c/Rosselló, 265, Dreta de l'Eixample, 08008
📞 +34 93 44 54 000
URL www.hotelomm.es

Room Mate Pau

🏠 c/Fontanella 7, Dreta de l'Eixample. 08010
📞 +34 93 34 36 300
URL pau.room-matehotels.com

Notes

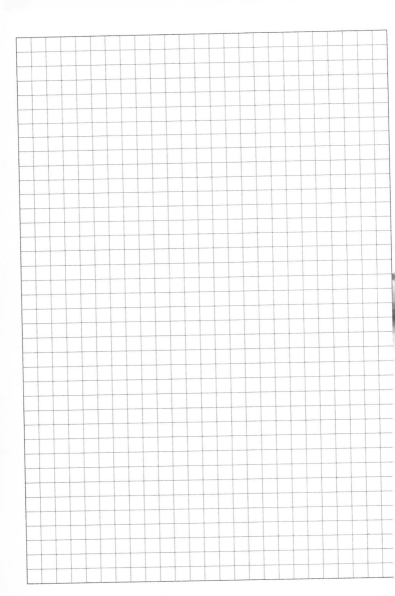

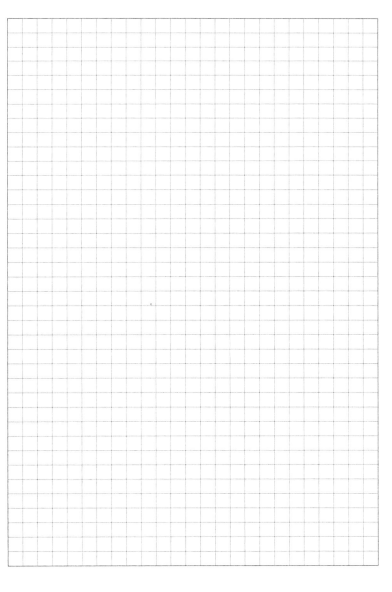

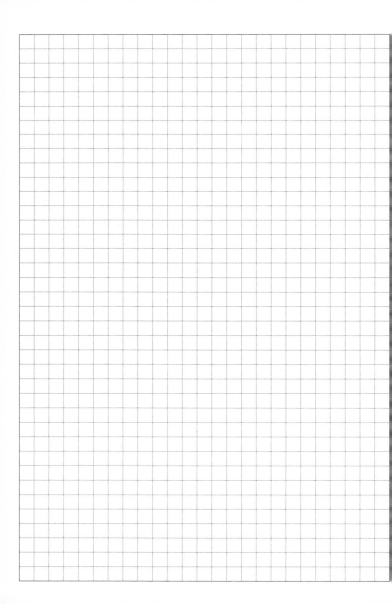